Get Ready
to explore!
The Great Outdoors

THE LIFE GRADUATE
PUBLISHING GROUP

Copyright 2020

NAME: _______________________________

AGE: _______________________________

ADDRESS: _______________________________

Add Your Photo Here

SAFETY IN THE WIILDERNESS

Pay attention to your trail. Some trails may have steep slopes, so be careful.

If you are wading through water and slippery cobbles, you could lose your footing. If wading, stick to very shallow areas with good footing.

Take more water than you think you will need. A sturdy drink bottle that will not break if dropped is important.

Take a phone with you. Communication in case of an emergency is important.

Always let someone else know where you plan to be exploring in the wilderness. If you don't return at the time you said you would, they can notify authorities accordingly.

Take a whistle to attract attention if needed

Keep up to date on the weather. Be mindful of forecast changes that may bring rain, wind or storms.

SAFETY IN THE WILDERNESS

While on the trail, take time to look back the way you've come. Trails look different when you turn around, and junctions are especially important places to get a picture in your mind of the way to go.

Carry Mapping Tools: You should carry a map and compass or a GPS, and know how to use them.

Wear the appropriate clothing and footwear for the conditions.

Take some high energy food bars or trail mix.

MY EXPLORING CHECKLIST

☐ Water	☐ Food/Snacks
☐ Whistle	☐ Backpack
☐ Map/GPS system	☐ Comfortable Footwear
☐ Phone	☐ Binoculars
☐ Pencil/Pens	☐ Plastic Container *Collecting Samples

☐ *My Exploring Nature Journal!*

DATE / /

START TIME : AM/PM **END TIME** : AM/PM

LOCATION DETAILS ____

____

WEATHER CONDITIONS _______________________________________

OBSERVATIONS AND FIELD NOTES

....

....

....

....

....

....

....

....

OTHER NOTES

....

....

....

....

....

....

WHAT DID YOU SEE?

Record Your Drawings, Add Photos or Anything Else Here

DATE   / /

START TIME   :   AM/PM   END TIME   :   AM/PM

LOCATION DETAILS ____

____

WEATHER CONDITIONS ____

OBSERVATIONS AND FIELD NOTES

OTHER NOTES

WHAT DID YOU SEE?

Record Your Drawings, Add Photos or Anything Else Here

DATE / /

START TIME : AM/PM **END TIME** : AM/PM

LOCATION DETAILS ____

____

WEATHER CONDITIONS _______________________________

OBSERVATIONS AND FIELD NOTES

....

....

....

....

....

....

....

....

OTHER NOTES

....

....

....

....

....

....

WHAT DID YOU SEE?

Record Your Drawings, Add Photos or Anything Else Here

DATE   / /

START TIME   :   AM/PM   END TIME   :   AM/PM

LOCATION DETAILS ____

____

WEATHER CONDITIONS ____

OBSERVATIONS AND FIELD NOTES

OTHER NOTES

WHAT DID YOU SEE?

Record Your Drawings, Add Photos or Anything Else Here

DATE   / /

START TIME   :   AM/PM   END TIME   :   AM/PM

LOCATION DETAILS ____

____

WEATHER CONDITIONS _______________________________________

OBSERVATIONS AND FIELD NOTES

....

....

....

....

....

....

....

....

OTHER NOTES

....

....

....

....

....

....

WHAT DID YOU SEE?

Record Your Drawings, Add Photos or Anything Else Here

DATE   /   /

START TIME   :   AM/PM   **END TIME**   :   AM/PM

LOCATION DETAILS ____

____

WEATHER CONDITIONS _______________________________________

OBSERVATIONS AND FIELD NOTES

....
....
....
....
....
....
....
....

OTHER NOTES

....
....
....
....
....
....

WHAT DID YOU SEE?

Record Your Drawings, Add Photos or Anything Else Here

DATE / /

START TIME : AM/PM **END TIME** : AM/PM

LOCATION DETAILS ____

____

WEATHER CONDITIONS ____

OBSERVATIONS AND FIELD NOTES

....

....

....

....

....

....

....

....

OTHER NOTES

....

....

....

....

....

....

WHAT DID YOU SEE?

Record Your Drawings, Add Photos or Anything Else Here

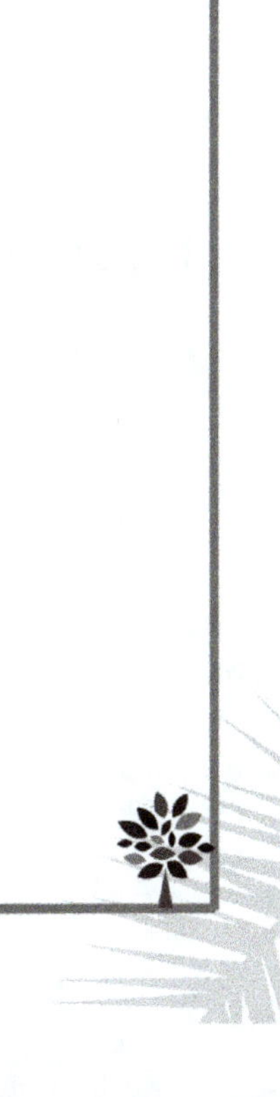

DATE   /   /

START TIME   :   AM/PM   END TIME   :   AM/PM

LOCATION DETAILS ____

____

WEATHER CONDITIONS ____

OBSERVATIONS AND FIELD NOTES

....

....

....

....

....

....

....

....

OTHER NOTES

....

....

....

....

....

....

WHAT DID YOU SEE?

Record Your Drawings, Add Photos or Anything Else Here

DATE   / /

START TIME   :   AM/PM   **END TIME**   :   AM/PM

LOCATION DETAILS _______________________________________

____

WEATHER CONDITIONS _______________________________

OBSERVATIONS AND FIELD NOTES

....
....
....
....
....
....
....
....

OTHER NOTES

....
....
....
....
....
....

WHAT DID YOU SEE?

Record Your Drawings, Add Photos or Anything Else Here

DATE   /   /

START TIME   :   AM/PM   **END TIME**   :   AM/PM

LOCATION DETAILS ____

____

WEATHER CONDITIONS ____

OBSERVATIONS AND FIELD NOTES

....
....
....
....
....
....
....
....

OTHER NOTES

....
....
....
....
....
....

WHAT DID YOU SEE?

Record Your Drawings, Add Photos or Anything Else Here

DATE / /

START TIME : AM/PM **END TIME** : AM/PM

LOCATION DETAILS ____

____

WEATHER CONDITIONS _______________________________________

OBSERVATIONS AND FIELD NOTES

....

....

....

....

....

....

....

....

OTHER NOTES

....

....

....

....

....

....

WHAT DID YOU SEE?

Record Your Drawings, Add Photos or Anything Else Here

DATE   /   /

START TIME   :   AM/PM   END TIME   :   AM/PM

LOCATION DETAILS ____

____

WEATHER CONDITIONS ____

OBSERVATIONS AND FIELD NOTES

....

....

....

....

....

....

....

....

OTHER NOTES

....

....

....

....

....

....

WHAT DID YOU SEE?

Record Your Drawings, Add Photos or Anything Else Here

DATE   /   /

START TIME   :   AM/PM   **END TIME**   :   AM/PM

LOCATION DETAILS ____

____

WEATHER CONDITIONS _______________________________________

OBSERVATIONS AND FIELD NOTES

....
....
....
....
....
....
....
....

OTHER NOTES

....
....
....
....
....
....

WHAT DID YOU SEE?

Record Your Drawings, Add Photos or Anything Else Here

DATE / /

START TIME : AM/PM   **END TIME** : AM/PM

LOCATION DETAILS ____

____

WEATHER CONDITIONS ____

OBSERVATIONS AND FIELD NOTES

....

....

....

....

....

....

....

....

OTHER NOTES

....

....

....

....

....

....

WHAT DID YOU SEE?

Record Your Drawings, Add Photos or Anything Else Here

DATE / /

START TIME : AM/PM **END TIME** : AM/PM

LOCATION DETAILS _______________________________________

____

WEATHER CONDITIONS _______________________________________

OBSERVATIONS AND FIELD NOTES

OTHER NOTES

WHAT DID YOU SEE?

Record Your Drawings, Add Photos or Anything Else Here

DATE / /

START TIME : AM/PM **END TIME** : AM/PM

LOCATION DETAILS _______________________________________

____

WEATHER CONDITIONS _______________________________________

OBSERVATIONS AND FIELD NOTES

....

....

....

....

....

....

....

....

OTHER NOTES

....

....

....

....

....

....

WHAT DID YOU SEE?

Record Your Drawings, Add Photos or Anything Else Here

DATE   /   /

START TIME   :   AM/PM   **END TIME**   :   AM/PM

LOCATION DETAILS ____

____

WEATHER CONDITIONS ______________________________________

OBSERVATIONS AND FIELD NOTES

....

....

....

....

....

....

....

....

OTHER NOTES

....

....

....

....

....

....

WHAT DID YOU SEE?

Record Your Drawings, Add Photos or Anything Else Here

DATE   /   /

START TIME   :   AM/PM   **END TIME**   :   AM/PM

LOCATION DETAILS ____

____

WEATHER CONDITIONS ____

OBSERVATIONS AND FIELD NOTES

....

....

....

....

....

....

....

....

OTHER NOTES

....

....

....

....

....

....

WHAT DID YOU SEE?

Record Your Drawings, Add Photos or Anything Else Here

DATE / /

START TIME   :   AM/PM   **END TIME**   :   AM/PM

LOCATION DETAILS _______________________________________

____

WEATHER CONDITIONS _______________________________________

OBSERVATIONS AND FIELD NOTES

....

....

....

....

....

....

....

....

OTHER NOTES

....

....

....

....

....

....

WHAT DID YOU SEE?

Record Your Drawings, Add Photos or Anything Else Here

DATE / /

START TIME : AM/PM   **END TIME** : AM/PM

LOCATION DETAILS _______________________________________

____

WEATHER CONDITIONS _______________________________________

OBSERVATIONS AND FIELD NOTES

....

....

....

....

....

....

....

....

OTHER NOTES

....

....

....

....

....

....

WHAT DID YOU SEE?

Record Your Drawings, Add Photos or Anything Else Here

DATE / /

START TIME : AM/PM   **END TIME** : AM/PM

LOCATION DETAILS _______________________________________

____

WEATHER CONDITIONS _______________________________________

OBSERVATIONS AND FIELD NOTES

....

....

....

....

....

....

....

....

OTHER NOTES

....

....

....

....

....

....

WHAT DID YOU SEE?

Record Your Drawings, Add Photos or Anything Else Here

DATE / /

START TIME : AM/PM **END TIME** : AM/PM

LOCATION DETAILS ____

____

WEATHER CONDITIONS ____

OBSERVATIONS AND FIELD NOTES

OTHER NOTES

WHAT DID YOU SEE?

Record Your Drawings, Add Photos or Anything Else Here

DATE   /   /

START TIME   :   AM/PM   END TIME   :   AM/PM

LOCATION DETAILS ____

____

WEATHER CONDITIONS ____

OBSERVATIONS AND FIELD NOTES

....

....

....

....

....

....

....

....

OTHER NOTES

....

....

....

....

....

....

WHAT DID YOU SEE?

Record Your Drawings, Add Photos or Anything Else Here

DATE   /   /

START TIME   :   AM/PM   **END TIME**   :   AM/PM

LOCATION DETAILS ____

____

WEATHER CONDITIONS ____

OBSERVATIONS AND FIELD NOTES

....

....

....

....

....

....

....

....

OTHER NOTES

....

....

....

....

....

....

WHAT DID YOU SEE?

Record Your Drawings, Add Photos or Anything Else Here

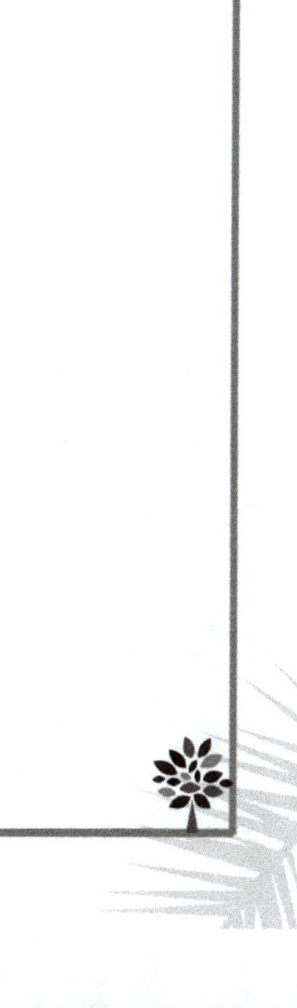

DATE   /   /

START TIME   :   AM/PM   **END TIME**   :   AM/PM

LOCATION DETAILS ____

____

WEATHER CONDITIONS ______________________________________

OBSERVATIONS AND FIELD NOTES

....

....

....

....

....

....

....

....

OTHER NOTES

....

....

....

....

....

....

WHAT DID YOU SEE?

Record Your Drawings, Add Photos or Anything Else Here

DATE / /

START TIME : AM/PM **END TIME** : AM/PM

LOCATION DETAILS ____

____

WEATHER CONDITIONS _______________________________________

OBSERVATIONS AND FIELD NOTES

....

....

....

....

....

....

....

....

OTHER NOTES

....

....

....

....

....

....

WHAT DID YOU SEE?

Record Your Drawings, Add Photos or Anything Else Here

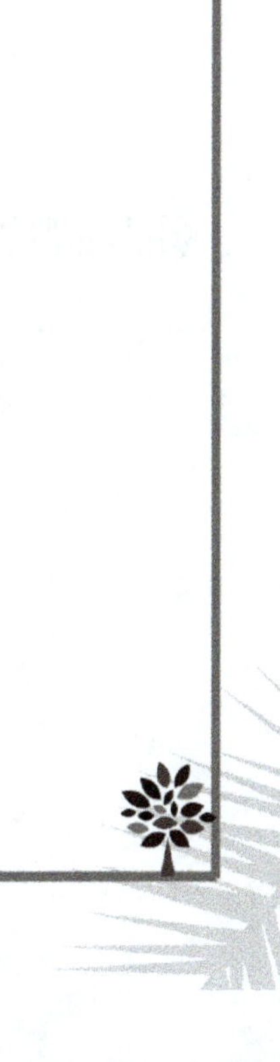

DATE   /   /

START TIME   :   AM/PM   **END TIME**   :   AM/PM

LOCATION DETAILS ____

____

WEATHER CONDITIONS ____

OBSERVATIONS AND FIELD NOTES

....

....

....

....

....

....

....

....

OTHER NOTES

....

....

....

....

....

....

WHAT DID YOU SEE?

Record Your Drawings, Add Photos or Anything Else Here

DATE / /

START TIME : AM/PM **END TIME** : AM/PM

LOCATION DETAILS _______________________________

____

WEATHER CONDITIONS _______________________________

OBSERVATIONS AND FIELD NOTES

OTHER NOTES

WHAT DID YOU SEE?

Record Your Drawings, Add Photos or Anything Else Here

DATE / /

START TIME : AM/PM **END TIME** : AM/PM

LOCATION DETAILS ____

____

WEATHER CONDITIONS ____

OBSERVATIONS AND FIELD NOTES

....

....

....

....

....

....

....

OTHER NOTES

....

....

....

....

....

....

WHAT DID YOU SEE?

Record Your Drawings, Add Photos or Anything Else Here

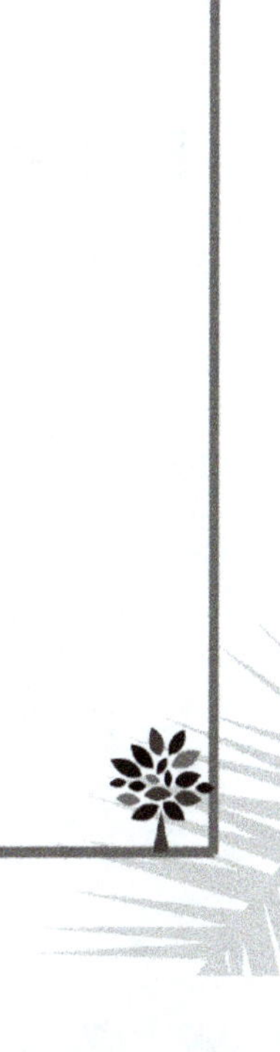

DATE / /

START TIME : AM/PM **END TIME** : AM/PM

LOCATION DETAILS ____

____

WEATHER CONDITIONS ______________________________________

OBSERVATIONS AND FIELD NOTES

....

....

....

....

....

....

....

....

OTHER NOTES

....

....

....

....

....

....

WHAT DID YOU SEE?

Record Your Drawings, Add Photos or Anything Else Here

DATE / /

START TIME : AM/PM **END TIME** : AM/PM

LOCATION DETAILS ____

____

WEATHER CONDITIONS _______________________________________

OBSERVATIONS AND FIELD NOTES

....

....

....

....

....

....

....

....

OTHER NOTES

....

....

....

....

....

....

WHAT DID YOU SEE?

Record Your Drawings, Add Photos or Anything Else Here

DATE   /   /

START TIME   :   AM/PM   END TIME   :   AM/PM

LOCATION DETAILS ____

____

WEATHER CONDITIONS ____

OBSERVATIONS AND FIELD NOTES

OTHER NOTES

WHAT DID YOU SEE?

Record Your Drawings, Add Photos or Anything Else Here

DATE / /

START TIME : AM/PM **END TIME** : AM/PM

LOCATION DETAILS ____

____

WEATHER CONDITIONS _______________________________________

OBSERVATIONS AND FIELD NOTES

....

....

....

....

....

....

....

....

OTHER NOTES

....

....

....

....

....

....

WHAT DID YOU SEE?

Record Your Drawings, Add Photos or Anything Else Here

DATE / /

START TIME : AM/PM **END TIME** : AM/PM

LOCATION DETAILS ___________________________________

____

WEATHER CONDITIONS ___________________________________

OBSERVATIONS AND FIELD NOTES

....
....
....
....
....
....
....
....

OTHER NOTES

....
....
....
....
....
....

WHAT DID YOU SEE?

Record Your Drawings, Add Photos or Anything Else Here

DATE   /   /

START TIME   :   AM/PM   END TIME   :   AM/PM

LOCATION DETAILS ____

____

WEATHER CONDITIONS ____

OBSERVATIONS AND FIELD NOTES

....
....
....
....
....
....
....
....

OTHER NOTES

....
....
....
....
....
....

WHAT DID YOU SEE?

Record Your Drawings, Add Photos or Anything Else Here

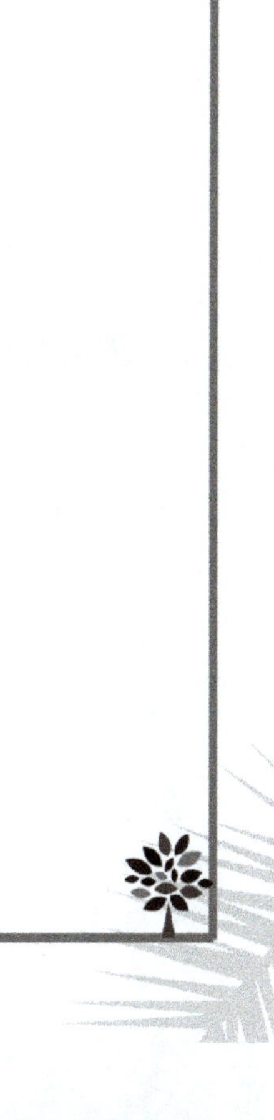

DATE   / /

START TIME   :   AM/PM   END TIME   :   AM/PM

LOCATION DETAILS ____

____

WEATHER CONDITIONS ______________________________________

OBSERVATIONS AND FIELD NOTES

....

....

....

....

....

....

....

....

OTHER NOTES

....

....

....

....

....

....

WHAT DID YOU SEE?

Record Your Drawings, Add Photos or Anything Else Here

DATE / /

START TIME : AM/PM **END TIME** : AM/PM

LOCATION DETAILS ____

____

WEATHER CONDITIONS _______________________________________

OBSERVATIONS AND FIELD NOTES

....

....

....

....

....

....

....

....

OTHER NOTES

....

....

....

....

....

....

WHAT DID YOU SEE?

Record Your Drawings, Add Photos or Anything Else Here

DATE   / /

START TIME   :   AM/PM   END TIME   :   AM/PM

LOCATION DETAILS ____

____

WEATHER CONDITIONS _______________________________________

OBSERVATIONS AND FIELD NOTES

....
....
....
....
....
....
....
....

OTHER NOTES

....
....
....
....
....
....

WHAT DID YOU SEE?

Record Your Drawings, Add Photos or Anything Else Here

DATE / /

START TIME : AM/PM **END TIME** : AM/PM

LOCATION DETAILS ____

____

WEATHER CONDITIONS _______________________________________

OBSERVATIONS AND FIELD NOTES

....

....

....

....

....

....

....

....

OTHER NOTES

....

....

....

....

....

WHAT DID YOU SEE?

Record Your Drawings, Add Photos or Anything Else Here

DATE / /

START TIME : AM/PM   **END TIME** : AM/PM

LOCATION DETAILS _______________________________

____

WEATHER CONDITIONS _______________________________

OBSERVATIONS AND FIELD NOTES

OTHER NOTES

WHAT DID YOU SEE?

Record Your Drawings, Add Photos or Anything Else Here

DATE   /   /

START TIME   :   AM/PM   END TIME   :   AM/PM

LOCATION DETAILS ____

____

WEATHER CONDITIONS ____

OBSERVATIONS AND FIELD NOTES

....
....
....
....
....
....
....
....

OTHER NOTES

....
....
....
....
....
....

WHAT DID YOU SEE?

Record Your Drawings, Add Photos or Anything Else Here

DATE / /

START TIME : AM/PM **END TIME** : AM/PM

LOCATION DETAILS ______________________________________

____

WEATHER CONDITIONS ______________________________

OBSERVATIONS AND FIELD NOTES

OTHER NOTES

WHAT DID YOU SEE?

Record Your Drawings, Add Photos or Anything Else Here

DATE   /   /

START TIME   :   AM/PM   **END TIME**   :   AM/PM

LOCATION DETAILS ____

____

WEATHER CONDITIONS __________________________________

OBSERVATIONS AND FIELD NOTES

OTHER NOTES

WHAT DID YOU SEE?

Record Your Drawings, Add Photos or Anything Else Here

DATE   /   /

START TIME   :   AM/PM   END TIME   :   AM/PM

LOCATION DETAILS ____

____

WEATHER CONDITIONS ____

OBSERVATIONS AND FIELD NOTES

....
....
....
....
....
....
....
....

OTHER NOTES

....
....
....
....
....
....

WHAT DID YOU SEE?

Record Your Drawings, Add Photos or Anything Else Here

DATE   /   /

START TIME   :   AM/PM   **END TIME**   :   AM/PM

LOCATION DETAILS ____

____

WEATHER CONDITIONS ________________________________

OBSERVATIONS AND FIELD NOTES

....
....
....
....
....
....
....
....

OTHER NOTES

....
....
....
....
....
....

WHAT DID YOU SEE?

Record Your Drawings, Add Photos or Anything Else Here

DATE / /

START TIME : AM/PM **END TIME** : AM/PM

LOCATION DETAILS _______________________________________

____

WEATHER CONDITIONS _______________________________

OBSERVATIONS AND FIELD NOTES

OTHER NOTES

WHAT DID YOU SEE?

Record Your Drawings, Add Photos or Anything Else Here

DATE / /

START TIME : AM/PM **END TIME** : AM/PM

LOCATION DETAILS ____

____

WEATHER CONDITIONS ________________________________

OBSERVATIONS AND FIELD NOTES

OTHER NOTES

WHAT DID YOU SEE?

Record Your Drawings, Add Photos or Anything Else Here

DATE   / /

START TIME   :   AM/PM   **END TIME**   :   AM/PM

LOCATION DETAILS _______________________________________

____

WEATHER CONDITIONS _______________________________________

OBSERVATIONS AND FIELD NOTES

....

....

....

....

....

....

....

....

OTHER NOTES

....

....

....

....

....

WHAT DID YOU SEE?

Record Your Drawings, Add Photos or Anything Else Here

I Love being in Nature!